Walking in the light

John Francis

BookLeaf Publishing

Presentation by *BookLeaf Publishing*

Web: www.bookleafpub.com

E-mail: info@bookleafpub.com

ISBN: 9789357441599

First edition 2023

DEDICATION

This goes out to my mom and dad. Thank you for all your love!

ACKNOWLEDGEMENT

I want to acknowledge my older brother Jordan for doing this first. I also want to give kudos to my parents for homeschooling me and instilling in me the capability to do this.

I want to acknowledge some references made

Dylan Thomas's Do Not Go Gently Into That Good Night in my work Light.

Marie Lu for the idea of Walking in the Light (the title) and the character of Day, which I reference in Pressure.

NeedToBreathe for their song Cages and Hurricane (I reference Hurricane in my poem Moment, and Cages in the poem Words)

Jesus and the Bible who I make references to numerous times

David Crowder for the song Forgiven which inspired me to write my own poem of the same name

Rick Riordan, who wrote the character of Percy Jackson that I reference in Words

Juice WRLD, who I reference with "999" (which is an actual tattoo I have) in the poem Empty House.

Regret

Nothing cuts so deep as regret
Broken glass rolling in your stomach as you realize
Those little, little cuts eating away at your soul
The blood dries
The words you said never to be taken back
Stinging your heart with the understanding
You made a deep mistake
Living a life of regret is no man's desire
All of us, however, feel the sting of it
What hope is there but to move on and not look back
To learn from those broken pieces
Step forward into the light

Light

It is said that one should not go gently into that good night
I say even more
Fight to preserve that light
The one that lives inside
Blowing on the spark occasionally
For you to realize
That inside you
Is someone asking, pleading, and knocking
For you to open that door
Hello
The one who waits for you wants you to know
You are loved, even in the depths
So, persevere
Hold on
Seek the light
Because when all is dark
The light shines the brightest

Beauty

Your beauty
Is not
Perfection
Your beauty
Is in
All the little imperfections
Of you
You are who you are
And there is beauty
in who you are
Thank you
For being
Beautiful

Void

So... I was talking to somebody last night

And the subject of the void entered our convo

We spoke of a desire

A desire to have the void.

This one's for you, kid.

The void.

The place where all

Is empty.

We know that there is no such place.

Yet

We long for it.

The pain is overwhelming.

What are we to do?

The pain

It's so hard.

To live.

To want anything but the removal of pain

How do we do it?

By strength of will

Then when that gives out

We return to one point

Our only hope

Our only hope to

To be free

Is not the void

I've been there

Where time and space are naught

No

Don't go there

To go there is to give up on the fight

To go there is to lose

To go there is to say

"There is nothing

Nothing but the pain

No one can

No one can help

Not family

Not friends

Not God himself"

You.

You know that's a bold-faced lie.

Get up

Continue

Renew yourself

When all is lost

When all is hopeless

And

You are curled up in a ball

Remember who's with you

FIGHT BACK!

AGAINST THE DARK!

AGAINST THE DEMONS OF HELL!

THAT LIVE INSIDE!

FIGHT BACK. C'MON!

Lift your head

Lift your head

Little warrior

Lift it child of the King

Do not give up

Do not give in to the idea

That the void

That it

That will remove your pain

It will not

I've been there

All the void does

Is make you cynical

Disbelieving that

Anyone is ever telling the truth

Unwilling to see the good

After which you have to recover

And remind yourself

That there is good

Keep fighting

You are a warrior

A king or queen

Someone who will not give up.

Don't stop till you are dead

Or

You've beaten them back

Do not. Give up.

You will always have measures of pain

It's what you do in those moments

That shows

Who you are.

Fight back. Or you've already lost.

Time

This is the end
Cars, humans, and things we no longer mend
Tis is the end.

Boys and girls no longer play
Laughter and joy are not heard anymore along the way
Tis is the end.

Bikes and tykes no longer ride
People do not take from animals their hide
Tis is the end.

Pop, pop, pop is not heard in the houses
Happiness is not roused
Tis is the end.

Life is short
Men no longer go out to port
Tis is the end.

Never Give Up

It's going to be hard
Never give up
It's too scary
Never give up
It hurts
Never give up
I am going to die
Never give up
We are in our darkest time
Never give up even in the time of great darkness

Moment

In a moment.
Warning bells toll.
Time to run.
Time to break the path of our fathers.
Hurricane.
You must run.
In the dawn.
In the evening.
You must.
Can the people be wiped clean?
Can you hear the warning bells?
Can you break the paradigm?

Dog

My coat was once glistening
My bones strong
My body able to fight for what is right
My teeth like that of a lion

Now I am old and weak
My coat not as shiny as it was, my hair starting
to grey and fall out
My bones weakening
My body no longer full of youthful vigor
My teeth no longer sharp as lions'

Will you remember me when I am old?
Will you take care of me?
As I did you?
Will you give me respect and care?

Demon

Ain't no rest for the wicked
Must be why I'm still awake
Ain't no rest for the wicked
Must be why I can't sleep
Mind wanders
Aight
It's time
Let's talk then.
Reason and logic out
Why am I
The way I am
A puzzle in the dark
A piece missin
Put me together
Take me apart.
A destination with no map
A maze with no end
Find me.
A piece of art they say
A masterpiece created by God
Some say
Idk about that
EDS
Cleft lip
Cleft pallet
They all got me more like
A bike without a wheel

A car with no engine
A boat with a hole in it
People say I shouldna cussed
I'm sorry. What am I supposed to do?
Whitewash a tomb
Here're some daisies
Go decorate that grave
I got issues. Anger
Rage
They all a monster in the cage
Sometimes
Sometimes I let 'em out
Depression like a chain on my soul
Anxiety that small child inside that never leaves
No structure
No sanity
Not even very creative
Hey.
Maybe there's a reason I can't write for shit
My body's so messed up
Hey
Maybe my writing is so broken
Cause I'm so
Broken
Not sure
Can't handle my darkness?
Maybe you shoulda left when I said leave
Can't handle the demon of the man
Shoulda never crawled near the cage
Welcome to the horror show.

Introspection

Walking up the steps of regret
Mind haunted with visions of death
The old man and the scythe
What is the point of life
What is the point of death
Why is one so long and one so short
My mind replays the stories I've told
The battles I've fought and won
The battles I've fought and lost
As I lay here
In this bed
Of dirt and of dust
Who was I
What mattered to me
What were the things that made up
John.
What would I say given another chance
What would I do, given another moment
Who am I?

Forgiven

Face in hands
Shame written all over me like a stain
Those three little words
Impossible to believe
Impossible to see
What have I done?
Is it possible?
I look at me and I see the scars
I look at me and I see the cuts
The ones from the knife I hold
As I cut into myself
When I fail
Is it possible?
Is this real?
Do I deserve?
Three little words
I forgive you
Rain in a drought
Light in the darkest night
Because deserving or not
I've been given them
Now. And forever more
I'm not perfect
I'm still broken
On my way to healing

But I'm forgiven.
Therefore.
In light of this
I ask you. Realize
You're forgiven. Forgive yourself.
Extend those three words.
I forgive you.
Tetelestai
It is finished.
Forgiven you are.

Pressure

Knock, Knock, Knock
Everything on me
Weighing down
A stone on my neck
Mistakes and failures
Regrets and pain
All this pressure
All this pain
What's it for?
And yet
I am stronger than it
So now
I break
I breakthrough
I push back
They're tryna hold on
They're trying to pin me down
I'm not stopping
Not now.
Not ever
I'm Day
I'm the boy who walks in the light
I'm John, of the clan Francis
I don't give up
Press down hard

Hand me every crappy card you got
I’ll still play them like a master
Give me a bad set up
Make all my pieces, pawns
I’ll still conquer
I’ll still come out, a grandmaster.
Because.
I refuse to give in
No giving up. Now
It’s your move
Will you rise under the gun?
Will you walk with me?
Will you conquer with me?
Will you have my back as I have yours?
Or will you give up?
Will you knock your king over?
Surrender?
Rise under the gun and take what is ours.

Words

I don't know that I have the words to express all
that is in my head
Somedays
I don't know what's right
I don't care about what's wrong
Why am I the way I am?
I am who I am

Ehyeh 'Ăšer 'Ehyeh
Isn't that God's line?
Yeah.
But it applies
Who am I?
The words spillin out of my head
All a mess
All my best
Dark inside and out
Madness, they say
Anxiety and depression
Hungry lions prowling at my soul
Devil's inside
All these thoughts
All these words
Not a single moment
To rest

Never stopping
Never allowing me a moment of peace
Who am I?
I'm a broke-nosed fighter
Stuck in a cage
Of all my doubt and regret
Cause I can't stop
What's happenin up top
Nonstop and yet
Never payin the debt
Everybody thinks they got it
But they don't
What's it like?
Like a never endin hurricane
I'm friggen Percy Jackson and I got my own hurricane
The wind and the waves
They say that the wind and waves
Speak of a being greater than I?
Have they sat in the storm?
Have they heard the rush of the wind?
An army of old
Vs one man
This is my mind
This is the devil in his purest form
Fighting me with everything he has
All I want is to do good
Doubt and anger and pain
Regret and sorrow and sadness

Weariness
They eat at my soul
Cause every night
I look the devil in the face
He is me
I am him
For
I do not wear the horns of evil
Nor do I seek the destruction of others
However, as any human should
I have come to terms
With the monster that lives inside my soul

Understanding

I once thought I understood
The way of the world
A few spins
Everyday a win
Everybody but me
Being perfect
I thought I was alone
The wolves of doubt and anger
Eatin at my soul
I was the one carryin my own pack
Haunted
Hunted
My failures
Vultures picking at a person long gone
Revelation
Everyone is broken
We're all carryin a torch
We all 'ave a bag
Full of
Regret
Loss
Doubt
The 10-ton weights attached to us
No one is perfect
No one is exactly what we pretend to be

Yet
Supposedly that's ok
Supposedly
Even though it hurts
We can be real
Cause there's this being
Who says he loves us
Says he cares
I'm blind
Cause I don't see it
However,
My best friend
A man I trust…
Says this is so
Therefore
My next step is
Believing that I am loved.
Not because I am Worthy
Because others choose to

Empty House

An empty house
Vacancy
The lights are on, but no one is home
Gone.
We have all these words for loss and yet
Do we understand it?
I know I don't
Even as a Christian, a man on a mission
I know this world takes me by surprise and I don't
understand
Why it all happens?
But strangely in the midst of a loss I find
Whether by God knowingly or unknowingly
We ride on
Do we have questions?
Yes
Always.
Somehow though, we find it
The strength to walk and not grow faint
It's a funny thing, isn't it?
Sometimes
All we have is the strength to walk
One step
One moment
Day by day we make it.
Loss
Emptiness
Gone

It leaves a hole
One we'll never naturally fill
Without something holding me up
So long ago
I would have been crushed
Only by the love of others
And by the grace of God
Do I take that step
See, without him
I would falter
I would faint
Where was God when my cousin died?
I wondered that
Strangely I found the answer
In another person's words
Who, after losing a child, as I recall
Heard them from another person
Where was God? I reckon he was in the same place
When his own son died.
Rage
Scream
Cry
Weep
Understand, that he knows though
These words
See.
They aren't mine
Because in a month or three or less
Perhaps more even
Something will happen
I'll forget I wrote this
And I'll need this encouragement

And it'll be here
So, hear this.
Not from me John Francis
But from the one giving me the words
Does he understand your pain?
Yes
Does his heart break into a million pieces?
Yes
Does the amount of love he has for you eclipse the whole of the earth
Does his love shatter mountains with its strength
Does his love create galaxies
And shatter evil's plans?
Yes.
"John. You don't know what I'm feeling!"
No.
I don't. I don't even know what I'll be feeling
But.
Know this.
One broken person to another
One 23-year-old kid to whoever reads this
Are you a beloved of the most high?
He who shattered the plans of evil to return you to him
That he might show you the depths of his love
In spite of the most pitch black, 2 am darkness?
Yes.
I don't have the words
To ease the pain
Of the loss you feel
But please
Just know.

You're loved.
By someone who does not sleep
Who does not stop
Who always stays on task
Who's mind never wanders and
By one who knows you so intimately
He formed the very being of who you are.
"John! How can he care! How can he have formed
me? My body is so broken!"
My friend
I understand in a way I hope no one else will ever
have to
My friend, I get it
CSID
EDS
Osteoporosis
Depression
Anxiety
Those are just the medical demons I fight
And yet
Somewhere deep inside me, I know
I'm formed how I'm supposed to be
999/Genesis 50:20
It's one of my tattoos
"You intended to harm me
God intended it all for good.
He brought me to this position
That I could save the lives of many people."
See I get it
A broken jar is what I feel like sometimes
I know I could do so much more
Yet have all these issues that limit me

Why?
Somewhere deep inside
Though
I know
It's being used for his glory to my good
If not mine, then yours
Do I hate it? Am I angry a lot of times about this?
Do I wish there was some other way?
YES!
But
It's recorded that even the most high begged for a different outcome
"Jesus said to his disciples, "Sit here while I pray.
My soul is overwhelmed with sorrow to the point of death,
Abba,[a] Father," he said
"Everything is possible for you.
Take this cup from me.
Yet not what I will, but what you will"
He begged for a change of plans
I do too.
His cup changed the world.
I have no clue what God plans for me or you.
All I know is that, even in loss, even in pain
When there is nothing
He's on it, moving, walking the plain.

Last word

The last word.
The last thing you'll ever say.
What will be left at the end of the day?
Don't let the sun go down while you're angry
Isn't that what the Bible says?

No one will remember the mistakes you made
But they will recall those last words you said
But they will remember what they read
But they'll remember your love

Before I go
Know
I
love
you.
Don't leave this world without the last thing you say
Being the most important thing today

What will you leave behind?
I hope my last word is
That expression
Those three words
The ones with the most magic in the world
I. Love. You.

Lighthouse

Up on a hill
Resides an old lighthouse
Tall and bright
An old lighthouse
Years and years and years
Have passed by
And this old lighthouse
Has stood

Up on a hill
Resides an old lighthouse
Sailors and ships
Used to travel by
No longer
But the old lighthouse stands
Forever strong, never broken

Now
Every blue moon
An old yacht may pass
A schooner may grace
The waters near the lighthouse
Storms crash against
But still
The old lighthouse stands.

Truth and Lies

The masks we wear
The knives from our mouths
The acts we play
The lies we tell
The truths we hide
Lying within
Plastic without
Words like fire
Scalding people from within to burn those
outside
What is real?
Reality a simulation or a simulation reality
What is truth
What is the lie?
Hiding in the shadows to save a life
Or burning in the sun, a most honorable death

Shadow

The scars of the fallen
The words of the lost
Haunted and damned
Are we
The ones left behind
Their love left in our mind
Our ghosts go before
Alone through the last door
Their words
Their actions
Imprints on reality
Left within us
May we never
Lose them
Living on forever
Their spirit will go
But they will stay
Their shadow casting
Across the worlds
Who they were
Left with us
Til the end
Til the end
Til the end
Forevermore

Soul of the Adventurer

The wandering soul
The adventurous spirit.
The great mystery
Falling deeper into everything
Flying under the sky
The great game of life calls
It calls to those with adventure
It calls to those with beauty

Serpents

Scaly skin
Long green and gold bodies
Searching for things to eat
Yet to the land dwellers, their existence a feat
What great mysteries
the leviathan
searchers and seekers
Wandering souls never understood
captured and taken, each of their brood
for the hide and the meat.

www.ingramcontent.com/pod-product-compliance
Lightning Source LLC
Chambersburg PA
CBHW051747130826
49812CB00033B/1033
9789357441599